MAKING
MOVIES

Movie Acting

by Geoffrey M. Horn

GARETH**STEVENS**
GS
PUBLISHING
A Member of the WRC Media Family of Companies

Please visit our Web site at: www.garethstevens.com
For a free color catalog describing our list of high-quality books,
call 1-800-542-2595 (USA) or 1-800-387-3178 (Canada).

Library of Congress Cataloging-in-Publication Data

Horn, Geoffrey M.
    Movie acting / by Geoffrey M. Horn.
       p. cm. — (Making movies)
    Includes bibliographical references and index.
    ISBN-10: 0-8368-6836-6   ISBN-13: 978-0-8368-6836-4 (lib. bdg.)
    1. Motion picture acting—Juvenile literature. I. Title.
    II. Series: Horn, Geoffrey M. Making movies.
    PN1995.9.A26H67   2007
    791.43'028—dc22   2006004286

This edition first published in 2007 by
Gareth Stevens Publishing
A Weekly Reader® Company
1 Reader's Digest Road
Pleasantville, NY 10570-7000 USA

This edition copyright © 2007 by Gareth Stevens, Inc.

Concept: Sophia Olton-Weber
Managing Editor: Valerie J. Weber
Art direction and design: Tammy West
Picture research: Diane Laska-Swanke

Photo credits: Cover, © Walt Disney/courtesy Everett Collection;
p. 4 © MGM/courtesy Everett Collection; p. 5 © Paramount/courtesy
Everett Collection; pp. 6, 27 © Everett Collection; p. 7 © New Line/
courtesy Everett Collection; p. 8 © MGM/Everett Collection; p. 11
© Universal Pictures/courtesy Everett Collection; p. 12 Warner
Brothers/Photofest; p. 14 © Columbia/courtesy Everett Collection; p. 16
© 20th Century Fox/courtesy Everett Collection; p. 17 Miramax/Photofest;
p. 21 © Warner Brothers/courtesy Everett Collection; p. 22 © Miramax/
courtesy Everett Collection; pp. 23, 29 © Universal/courtesy Everett
Collection; p. 25 Pathe/Photofest; p. 26 © Universal/Everett Collection

Printed in the United States of America

 4 5 6 7 8 9 10 09 08 07

Contents

Cover: Johnny Depp portrays Jack Sparrow in *Pirates of the Caribbean: The Curse of the Black Pearl.*

Film Casting

Here's the scene: You're an experienced filmmaker. You've come up with a great idea for a movie. The sets, the costumes, the special effects, the music — you know exactly what you want. The head of a major studio has agreed to see you. You have five minutes to make your pitch. You describe the movie you have in mind.

"Interesting," says the studio head. "Who are the stars?" "I'm thinking Jamie Foxx and Beyoncé Knowles," you answer. "Fantastic," the studio exec replies. "Get me Jamie and Beyoncé, and you've got yourself a movie."

Beyoncé Knowles and Steve Martin added star power to the 2006 remake of *The Pink Panther.*

CELEBRITY SNAPSHOT
Angelina Jolie

Born: June 4, 1975, in Los Angeles, California

Film Career: Actress, producer

Academy Awards: Winner as supporting actress for *Girl, Interrupted* (1999)

Other Top Films: *Lara Croft: Tomb Raider; Mr. and Mrs. Smith*

Backstory: Jolie trained hard to play Lara Croft. But she feels the biggest challenge was capturing the character's inner strength. "Sometimes it's easier to be crazy . . . dark and inside yourself," she says. "For a year, I had to exercise every morning, be positive, be front and center and smiling. It was difficult for me."

Angelina Jolie treks through an African landscape in *Lara Croft Tomb Raider: The Cradle of Life*. Behind her is Djimon Hounsou.

Star Power

Stars give movies much of their power and glamour. One of the first screen idols was Rudolph Valentino. In the early 1920s, women flocked to theaters to see him in *The Sheik* and *Blood and Sand*. When he died at the age of thirty-one in 1926, huge screaming crowds came to his funeral. He was the Elvis of his era.

In the early 1920s, movie fans swooned at the sight of Rudolph Valentino in *The Sheik*.

Each generation has its own stars. During the 1940s and 1950s, Marilyn Monroe and Humphrey Bogart drew millions to the movies. Paul Newman, Robert Redford, and Jane Fonda became major stars during the 1970s. Today, Angelina Jolie, Julia Roberts, and George Clooney are famous worldwide.

What Makes Stars Different

About thirty thousand people in the United States have paying jobs as movie actors. Only a handful of them are stars. The top stars can get up to $20 million a movie. But on average, most actors earn less than someone who works in a clothing store.

Star quality is hard to define. But movie people —
and audiences — know it when they see it. When
the cameras start filming, star performers light up
the screen. Like magnets, they attract and hold
your attention. You laugh at them, cry with them,
and cheer for them.

Leading and Supporting Roles

Most movies have one or two stars. They play the
leading roles. The story usually focuses on what
they do and say.

Other parts are called supporting roles. These
supporting roles have different names depending
on their importance. If the supporting part is very
important, it is called a featured role. A bit part
is a very small role. An even smaller role is
known as a walk-on. People with smallest roles
are called extras.
They appear in
large groups
and crowds.

Colin Farrell was already
a star when he played
Captain John Smith in
The New World. Critics
hailed Q'Orianka Kilcher
— the teenage girl who
played Pocahontas — as
a star of the future.

Behind the Scenes:

What Is Typecasting?

When making a movie, directors often like to cast certain "types." Looking for an action hero? For decades, the answer was Arnold Schwarzenegger or Harrison Ford. Need a sexy, ditzy blonde? No one played that part better than Marilyn Monroe. Some actors are happy taking the same kind of role in film after film. Character actors often make a good living playing certain types of parts. For example, Steve Buscemi often plays sneaks, crooks, and crazies.

Typecasting can be a serious problem when it stems from narrow ideas about particular groups, however. For a long time, leading roles almost always went to white actors. Talented African American actors had a hard time getting good parts. Today, Asian, Latino, and Arab American actors also complain about being cast as particular types. They say they should be given a chance to show their talents in many different kinds of roles.

Some films with very low budgets have no stars. They use lesser-known actors in the main roles. Other movies have ensemble (ahn-SAHM-bull) casts. *Ensemble* comes from a French word meaning "together." An ensemble cast is one where the actors share the credit. Stars in an ensemble film may agree to take less than their usual pay because they want to appear in the movie.

Reese Witherspoon shatters the "dumb blonde" stereotype in *Legally Blonde*.

From the Stage to the Screen

Have you ever seen a really old movie? The stars don't act the way most actors do today. In early movies, their motions are larger than life. The movements of their faces are more intense than those in real life. As you watch, you may be sitting only a few feet from your TV screen. But most actors in very old movies look like they're acting for an audience that's a hundred feet away.

Many words describe this kind of over-acting. Some people call it hammy. Others call it melodramatic. The simple truth is, it feels fake. Today, actors are trained not to overact in serious movies. One well-known acting coach tells his students to watch their favorite performers. "You will see that they do very little," he writes. "Yet we know everything that is going on behind their faces. . . . It boils down to one thing: play the

Behind the Scenes:
Small Screen and Big Screen

When TV began, many movie people felt the small screen was for small talents. Movie stars rarely appeared on TV shows, and TV stars were rarely given the chance to star in movies. Today, that gap no longer exists. Many of today's stars, from Jamie Foxx to Hilary Duff, got their start on TV. Kiefer Sutherland has starred both in movies and on TV. So has Geena Davis.

Comic actors often use TV as a training ground. Steve Martin did stand-up comedy and TV work before he became a film actor, director, and screenwriter. Many movie comics launched their careers on TV with *Saturday Night Live*. Standouts include Eddie Murphy, Mike Myers, Will Ferrell, and Adam Sandler.

truth. Don't exaggerate. . . . Be simple."

Acting for the Camera
Screen acting differs from stage acting in many ways. For example, stage actors must be seen and heard in all parts of a large theater. Even in quiet scenes, they must speak loudly enough to be heard from far away. After all, the people in the balcony have to hear them.

Screen actors face a different problem. They perform in front of cameras that may be close enough to touch. In a close-up shot, tiny movements of their eyes and mouth are visible on the big screen. On a movie set, unseen microphones record the actors' voices. They can speak the way they would in real life.

Movies with special effects pose a challenge for the actors. In the *Jurassic Park* films, for example, the performers must act like fierce dinosaurs are chasing them. But the actors never see them. The fake dinosaurs aren't added to the film until much later. To show real terror, the actors must draw deeply on their own memories and feelings. They must find a time in their own lives when they were scared, then show that fear on-screen.

Sam Neill acts like he's running for his life in this shot from *Jurassic Park*. But there weren't any dinosaurs until director Steven Spielberg added them in the editing room.

CELEBRITY SNAPSHOT
Denzel Washington

Born: December 28, 1954, in Mount Vernon, New York

Film Career: Actor, producer, director

Academy Awards: Won for best supporting actor in *Glory* (1989) and best actor for *Training Day* (2001)

Other Top Films: *Cry Freedom*; *Malcolm X*; *The Hurricane*; *Antwone Fisher*

Backstory: After years of working in TV and movies, Washington performed in a play by William Shakespeare in 2005. He starred as Brutus in *Julius Caesar*. He told a reporter that stage acting was much harder than screen acting. But he liked being on stage because of the actors' contact with the audience. "You do a film, you get a crew of two hundred," he said. "They're used to doing films. You move on. You don't really interact with people too much. . . . There's nothing like the theater. You find out every night whether they like you or not."

Spike Lee (left) directed Denzel Washington in *Malcolm X*.

Beginnings and Endings

Stage actors go through the whole play at every performance. They begin at the beginning and end at the end. They must know every page of dialogue. They can build their characters from the very first line to the last.

Here again, movies are different. Almost all films are shot out of order. The last scenes might be filmed first, and the early scenes might be shot last. A film actor may need to memorize only a page or two of dialogue each day.

Why film this way? The answer is money. Suppose a screenplay has twenty scenes. The action switches back and forth between four different parts of the world: Hong Kong, Paris, New York, and Hollywood. To film the script in the right order, the cast and crew would have to keep flying from one city to the next. It's much faster and cheaper to film all the Hong Kong scenes first, then all the Paris scenes, and so forth.

Not all screen actors are happy with this way of working. Cameron Diaz complains that she never really understands the role she's playing until she finishes the shoot. "At the end of the movie," she says, "you're like: Can I do it again, please? Let me play it. I know what I'm going

Cameron Diaz (left), Drew Barrymore, and Lucy Liu go undercover as shipyard workers in a scene from *Charlie's Angels: Full Throttle.*

to do now. I know how to play the character.
I know what her story is. I know how to do
this now. Give me another chance!"

Basics of Film Acting

For most actors, the first step in getting a role is a screen test, or audition. An audition is a tryout. If you go to an audition, you will be required to read some lines aloud. You may be told to read alone or with someone else. Your audience will probably include the casting director. This person is in charge of finding the right actors for a particular film. The film director may also be present.

The Audition

The filmmakers will judge you on several things. The first is how you look. An actor needs to look right for the part. For example, if the character is young, the actor can't look too old.

The filmmakers will want to know how well you read — and how well you listen. You need to read your lines with feeling and understanding. You also need to look up from the script as often as you can, so the filmmakers can see your eyes and

CELEBRITY SNAPSHOT

Claire Danes

Born: April 12, 1979, in New York City

Film Career: Actress

Other Top Films: *Romeo + Juliet; The Hours; Shopgirl*

Backstory: Danes says she decided she wanted to be a performer when she was five years old, after seeing Madonna on TV. She was fifteen when she starred in TV's *My So-Called Life.* She won a Golden Globe Award (1995) for playing a high school student in the series.

Clare Danes played Juliet and Leonardo DiCaprio was Romeo in a 1996 film version of Shakespeare's tragic love story.

face. When not speaking, you need to listen carefully to the person who reads along with you. Filmmakers want to see how quickly you react to what other characters say. They also want to see if you understand the role you're reading for.

Shooting a Scene

When people watch a movie, they see only what the camera sees. What the camera shoots is called the frame. Anything inside the frame can be seen on the movie screen — and nothing else.

Consider this romantic scene. A man and a woman are sitting next to each other on a sofa. As they move closer together, their faces fill the screen. Their eyes close. Their lips touch. They kiss.

Here is what the movie audience doesn't see. Bright lights are strung up all over the set. Members of the film crew are everywhere. The director calls out instructions. The cameras start rolling, or filming. A sound person holds a

Cast and crew crowd the set of *Bride and Prejudice*. A microphone is held aloft on a boom, as director Gurinder Chadha (center, in pink) gives instructions.

Behind the Scenes:
Film Acting Awards

The best-known film acting prizes are the Academy Awards. These awards are also called Oscars. There are four acting Oscars: for best actor and actress in a leading role and for best supporting actor and actress.

Golden Globe Awards are given for acting in films and on TV. Unlike the Oscars, the Golden Globe voters choose one group of winners for dramas and another group of winners for musicals or comedies. The Screen Actors Guild (SAG) also gives awards each year. SAG is a labor union that seeks better pay and working conditions for film and TV performers.

microphone attached to a long pole, or "boom," above the actors' heads. The actors have to ignore all this noise and activity and focus only on themselves and each other.

Hitting Your Marks

In most movies, every shot is set up carefully. The lights and cameras are positioned precisely. As an actor, you must speak your lines correctly. But you must also move in exactly the right way. In rehearsals, the director will tell you where to move. Sometimes the floor of the set will be marked with tape to show you where you need to go. When you move correctly, you are said to be "hitting your marks."

Each scene done while the cameras are rolling is called a "take." Sometimes the director is satisfied with the first or second take. When that happens, the actors stop, and crew members set up the next scene.

More often, a scene must be redone several times before the director is happy with it. These repeated scenes are known as retakes. Actors must be able to do take after take without losing their focus.

Types of Shots

Directors and camera operators can choose from many types of shots. When doing a scene, actors need to know the kind of shot the director wants.

In a full shot, the actor's whole body is inside the frame. The audience can see everything the actor does. An extreme close-up is just the opposite. Only a small part of the actor can be seen. In a typical film, this might be the actor's eyes or one hand holding a pen or a gun.

The "two-shot" is very common in movies. Two-shots often show two people talking. In movies, people in two-shots usually stand closer to each other than they would in real life. This is so both actors can fit within the frame without wasting a lot of screen space.

In real life, people usually face each other when they talk. In movies, actors are expected to "cheat" by not facing each other directly. Instead, they may angle their faces toward the camera. With the actors in this position, the audience can get a better view of both faces.

CHAPTER 4

Meeting Special Challenges

When you're a film actor, you need to prepare for every role. Of course, you need to read the script and memorize your lines. But that is only the first step. You also need to understand why your character behaves in a particular way.

For example, suppose you're in a drama about the Civil Rights movement. You might start by reading about Dr. Martin Luther King, Jr. Have you ever been a victim of prejudice? How did you feel? What did you do about it? Questions like these can help you understand the motivations of the character you're playing.

Sharpening Skills

Different roles require different skills. For a movie about knights, you may need to learn how to ride a horse and fight with a sword. For a film about a shipwreck, you may need to work on swimming and diving. For a film set in a foreign country, you

CELEBRITY SNAPSHOT
Hilary Swank

Born: July 30, 1974, in Lincoln, Nebraska

Film Career: Actress, producer

Academy Awards: Won as best actress for *Boys Don't Cry* (1999) and *Million Dollar Baby* (2004)

Other Top Films: *Insomnia*

Backstory: Swank was a champion swimmer and gymnast when she was growing up. Her sports ability helped her prepare for her role as a boxer in *Million Dollar Baby*. Before filming began, she worked out at a gym. She gained nearly 20 pounds (9 kilograms) of muscle.

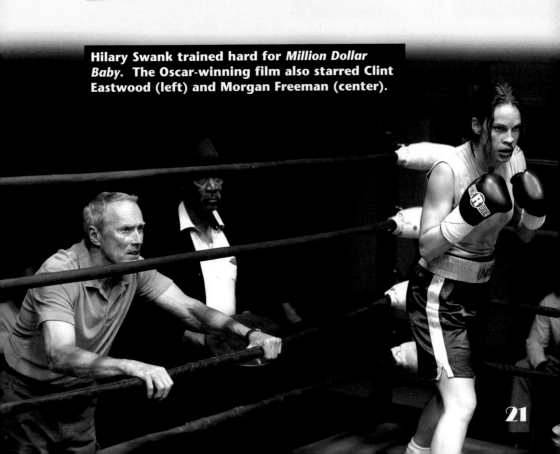

Hilary Swank trained hard for *Million Dollar Baby*. The Oscar-winning film also starred Clint Eastwood (left) and Morgan Freeman (center).

may need to sound like someone from that country.

When preparing for a role, actors often seek help from trainers and coaches. For example, Lucy Liu, Cameron Diaz, and Drew Barrymore spent three months in martial-arts training before making *Charlie's Angels*. The stars of *Chicago* rehearsed their music and dance numbers for six weeks. "I worked really hard before and during rehearsals," said *Chicago* star Catherine Zeta-Jones. "Some days I could hardly walk."

Actors from other countries may work with voice coaches on movies made in the United States. For example, Russell Crowe and Heath Ledger grew up in Australia. Voice coaches have helped both men sound more American.

Familiar Faces, Unusual Training
Many films tell stories about well-known people. These movies are sometimes called biopics (BY-oh-pix). Jamie Foxx starred in *Ray*, a biopic about Ray Charles. Foxx faced a complex challenge.

He had to walk, talk, and sing like one of the top names in the history of American music. He also had to play someone who was blind for most of his life.

Foxx spent many days with his eyes covered, learning what it felt like to be blind. The actor also met Ray Charles before filming began. His hard work paid off. On screen, Foxx gave an Oscar-winning performance as the great soul singer.

Behind the Scenes:
So You Want to Be a Movie Actor . . . ?

Most actors find that the more acting they do, the more they enjoy it. Even if you're shy in daily life, you may feel an energy rush when the camera starts rolling. Start by writing and performing short plays with your family. Buy or borrow a video camera and make short films with your friends. Take drama classes in school. Join an after-school drama club. See as many plays and movies as you can.

More than two hundred U.S. colleges and universities grant degrees in acting. One of the best-known acting schools is the Lee Strasberg Theatre and Film Institute. The school holds classes in Los Angeles and New York City.

Jamie Foxx was convincing as Ray Charles.

CHAPTER 5

Make 'Em Laugh!

Here's an old story. Maybe you've heard it. An elderly comedian is on his deathbed. All of his friends surround him. Some of them are crying. "This must be so hard for you," one friend says. "Nah," the comic answers. "Dying is easy. Comedy is hard."

Movie comedy is different from stand-up comedy in front of an audience. Stand-up comics control their own act. Their audience tells them all they need to know. If a joke is really funny, the audience screams with laughter. If a joke bombs, the silence feels endless.

In a movie, the director — not the comic — controls the timing. The setup for a joke might be filmed one day. The punch line might be filmed the next. Months later, the film will be edited and screened for a test audience. Then, and only then, will the comic know how well the jokes work.

Comedy Classics

Comics have been top screen stars since the early days of movies. Harold Lloyd became known as the "Daredevil Comic." In one famous scene from his 1923 film *Safety Last*, he appears to dangle from a clock on top of a tall building. Charlie Chaplin's best-known character was the "Little Tramp." This character with sad eyes, mustache, baggy pants, and oversized shoes became world famous. Buster Keaton was called "The Great Stone Face." He kept his deadpan look while crazy things happened all around him.

One of the most famous shots in movie history — Harold Lloyd's daredevil dangle.

25

CELEBRITY SNAPSHOT

Ben Stiller

Born: November 30, 1965, in New York City

Film Career: Actor, producer, director, screenwriter

Top Films: *There's Something About Mary; Meet the Parents; Zoolander; Dodgeball; Madagascar*

Backstory: Ben Stiller is the son of two comic actors, Jerry Stiller and Anne Meara. Before he became a movie star, he had his own TV comedy series, *The Ben Stiller Show.* He takes comic acting very seriously. His wife, actress Christine Taylor, says, "He's not the class clown. . . . He doesn't even consider himself that funny."

Robert De Niro grills Ben Stiller in the "lie detector" scene from *Meet the Parents.*

Lucille Ball (right) appeared in dozens of movies before starring in the hit TV comedy series *I Love Lucy*. In this classic scene, Lucy takes a job in a candy factory.

One of the most popular screen comics of all time is Lucille Ball. Fifty years after they were made, her *I Love Lucy* shows are still TV favorites. Lily Tomlin and Goldie Hawn went from TV's *Laugh-In* to movie stardom. Julia Roberts and Sandra Bullock often choose comic roles.

To make sure their movies reflected their comic ideas, Chaplin and Keaton directed many of their own films. Later comics learned from their example. Woody Allen and Mel Brooks have written, directed, and starred in their own movies. So have Albert Brooks and Ben Stiller.

Behind the Scenes:
Playing Comic Types

One expert on comedy says that comic characters come in eight basic types. He gives these characters names like the Dumb One, the Logical Smart One, and the Lovable Loser. For example, on *The Simpsons*, the Dumb One is Homer. ("D'Oh!") The comic actor's first task is to know which type to play.

Some characters combine two or more types. That's how Reese Witherspoon plays Elle Woods in *Legally Blonde*. Other characters in the film look down on her as the Dumb One. But by the end, she turns out to be the Smart One.

Slapstick Comedy

As a comic, you can get laughs with witty lines and clever wordplay. You can also get laughs by making your face, voice, and body do silly things. Most movie comics rely on both verbal and physical skills.

Physical comedy is sometimes called slapstick. A good slapstick film is fast-paced, with lots of visual gags and wild action. The characters brawl, throw pies and other things, and may try to gross out each other in various ways. Adam Sandler and Jim Carrey specialize in this kind of comedy. Carrey is one of the best physical comics in movie history. Some of his most popular films are *Dumb and Dumber* and *Bruce Almighty*. Steve Martin has also shown great talent for both physical and verbal comedy.

Comedy stars are often overlooked when Oscar time rolls around. But they're some of the hardest-working and most talented actors in the movies. "People don't realize how much goes into comic acting," says acting teacher Michael Kahn. Like other actors, comics need to know their lines and hit their marks. They need to understand their characters and their craft. But unlike actors in straight dramas, they need to do all this hard work and make it look like fun!

A small comic miracle in *Bruce Almighty* — Jim Carrey uses his godlike powers to part a "red sea" of tomato soup.

Glossary

Academy Award — also called an Oscar; an award given out by the movie industry.

audition — a tryout in which an actor reads for a role.

backstory — the background story to something seen on screen.

biopics — films based on the lives of famous people.

deadpan — showing no emotion.

dialogue — in a screenplay or play, the words the characters say to each other.

director — the person who controls the creative part of making a movie.

frame — the boundary that separates what can be seen on screen from what cannot; also the separate photographs that make up a movie.

marks — instructions, often shown by tape on the floor, that tell the actors where to move

motivations — a character's reasons for behaving in a particular way.

pitch — sales presentation of a film idea to a studio head.

punch line — in a joke, the line at the end that triggers the biggest laugh.

stand-up comedy — jokes or funny comments delivered in front of a live audience.

take — in movies, a scene done while the cameras are rolling.

To Find Out More

Books

An Actor. I Want to Be (series). Ivan Bulloch and Diana James (Two-Can Publishers)

Break a Leg! The Kid's Guide to Acting and Stagecraft. Lisa Friedman (Workman Publishing)

Lights, Camera, Action!: Making Movies and TV from the Inside Out. Lisa O'Brien (Maple Tree Press)

Working in Film and Television. My Future Career (series). Margaret McAlpine (Gareth Stevens)

Videos

William Shakespeare's Romeo + Juliet (20th Century Fox) PG-13

Web Sites

Cinema: How Are Hollywood Films Made?
www.learner.org/exhibits/cinema/acting.html
Learn about what it takes to be a film actor

Academy of Motion Picture Arts and Sciences
www.oscars.org
Guide to the Academy Awards

AWOL: Acting Workshop Online
www.redbirdstudio.com/AWOL/acting2.html
A site about the business of acting

Publisher's note to educators and parents: Our editors have carefully reviewed these Web sites to ensure that they are suitable for children. Many Web sites change frequently, however, and we cannot guarantee that a site's future contents will continue to meet our high standards of quality and educational value. Be advised that children should be closely supervised whenever they access the Internet.

Index

About the Author

Geoffrey M. Horn has been a fan of music, movies, and sports for as long as he can remember. He has written more than three dozen books for young people and adults, along with hundreds of articles for encyclopedias and other works. He lives in southwestern Virginia, in the foothills of the Blue Ridge Mountains, with his wife, their collie, and four cats. He dedicates this book to Wayne Bowman, Rex Stephenson, and community theaters everywhere.